Saved, Sanctified

and still need a drink!

A SELF DISCOVERY JOURNEY

BARBARA FREEMAN

Copyrighted Material

Saved, Sanctified and Still Need a Drink!

Copyright © 2015 by Sea Change Press. All Rights Reserved.

No part of this publication may be reproduced, stored in a retrieval system or transmitted, in any form or by any means—electronic, mechanical, photocopying, recording or otherwise—without prior written permission from the publisher, except for the inclusion of brief quotations in a review.

For information about this title or to order other books and/or electronic media, contact the publisher:
Sea Change Press
seachangepress@gmail.com

ISBN: 978-0-9965409-0-2

Printed in the United States of America
Cover and Interior design: 1106 Design

Dedication

To my father, Elder Charles A. Freeman
who passed away in 2011.
He used to always sing this song:

*"Farther Along, we'll know all about it.
Farther Along, we'll understand why.
Cheer up, my brother. Live in the sunshine.
We'll understand it, all by and by."*

Thank you, Dad…now, I finally get it!

TABLE OF CONTENTS

Tell the Truth! When You Saw the Title of this Book...   vii
Happy Hour!   ix
Introduction   1
Chapter 1:   White Zinfandel   7
Chapter 2:   Bloody Mary or Shirley Temple?   13
Chapter 3:   The Confession Bar   17
Chapter 4:   Old Fashioned or New School?   21
Chapter 5:   "Top Shelf" or "Off Brand"   25
Chapter 6:   This One's "On the House"   31
Chapter 7:   Straight, No Chaser   37
Chapter 8:   A Big Hangover   45
Chapter 9:   Flat Champagne   51
Chapter 10:   Invisible Drunks   55
Chapter 11:   Good Spirits   59
Chapter 12:   Eat, Drink, and Be Merry!   63
Chapter 13:   Not to Leave You Hanging—The Nightcap!   69

TELL THE TRUTH! WHEN YOU SAW THE TITLE OF THIS BOOK....

Did you laugh? If so, I suspect you already know what "saved" and "sanctified" mean, and that they're not supposed to go with "and still need a drink!" Unless, of course, it's a drink of "living water" from "the well that never runs dry"!

Did you feel offended? If so, you may think this book is going to be nothing but a bunch of foolishness by someone who doesn't understand what it **means** to be "saved and sanctified"!

Did you see the makings of a *"Madea Goest to Rehab"* style comedy or play? Surely there is a Tyler Perry character you recognize in your head that aptly matches the title.

Did you think it could be about *Recovering Alcoholics in the Holiness Church*? You may be curious about that topic. Especially since you've never seen a book about it before. Saved and sanctified people and alcoholism. Really?

Did you feel afraid to even pick up this book? Did it spark twinges of condemnation about your own behavior that you know goes against your church's teachings? You know what I mean!

Just like buying a bootleg movie, did you feel a little *guilty pleasure*? What might a book like this reveal about the "dirty laundry" inside of the world of the "saved and sanctified?" Do some preachers really have wet bars hidden in their church offices?

Well, guess what? I also felt these hypothetical reactions, but the main one I thought was *"Ooh, no! I didn't go there!"* And I'm the one who wrote the book!

So much is implied in just the title alone, isn't it? It piques curiosity, raises questions, and stirs deep-seated feelings. Most of all, it gets your attention! So if you are still reading, I assume you are ready to see what I am talking about. Don't worry—it's all good!

To get you in the mood, just take a deep breath, and if you're in the bookstore, or on your e-reader, just turn to the person closest to you and say:

> **"Neighbor, I'm about to read this book called *Saved, Sanctified…and Still Need a Drink!*"**

And see what kind of reaction you get!

HAPPY HOUR!

Consider this scenario. You just had a hard day at work, and you feel really frustrated and stressed out. You need to vent about your crazy boss, and, so, you call your best friend. "You won't believe my day! I need a *drink!*" Your friend agrees to meet up with you for Happy Hour after work, where you can order a drink, unwind, and debrief your hectic day.

Whether or not you drink alcohol, when you hear someone say, "I need a drink" it's usually because they're angry, frustrated, confused, or disappointed, and they either want to talk about it or do something out of character. We all have moments when we feel like that, right?

However, when any of your friends or colleagues communicate their feelings with statements like this...

> "Girlfriend, if I wasn't saved, I would cuss you out now and repent later!"

> "I need to be prayed up to deal with this mess..."

Saved, Sanctified and Still Need a Drink!

> *"If I didn't know the Lord, I would not hesitate to jack you up!"*
>
> *"You are just the Devil trying to steal my joy! Satan, the Lord rebuke you, in the name of Jesus!"*
>
> *"The Bible said, 'Thou shalt not kill'; it didn't say I couldn't shoot your kneecaps!"*
>
> *"I don't want to have to backslide over this, but I will if you keep it up!"*
>
> *"You are this close to making me lose my salvation!"*

…then just assume they come from the "saved and sanctified" church culture, and are letting you know "they need a drink!" How can you tell?

Notice the "code speak." The words **"saved," "prayed up," "the Lord," "the Devil," "the Bible," "salvation,"** are all mentioned in the same sentence as **"cuss you out," "jack you up," "shoot your kneecaps," "backsliding,"** and **"losing your salvation."**

Who else does that?

Actually, this scenario is very common, but it may not make sense unless you are familiar with the "code speak" of what I call the "saved and sanctified" church culture. This kind of talk is displayed perfectly in the character Madea that media mogul Tyler Perry created and acts out in his plays and films.

What makes Madea so popular? Madea represents the gun-toting, weed-smoking, cursing, and will "whip you and your kids" grandma who knows the "saved and sanctified" church culture and gets credit for telling it like it is in a way that is oddly appreciated and respected.

Happy Hour!

If you don't get it, you may think Madea is just a joke. She promotes child beating, gun violence, and drug usage and still goes to church every now and then. She believes "Jesus Saves" but doesn't claim salvation for herself, which justifies her ability to point out hypocrites like a laser beam. She makes fun of the saved and sanctified folks' quirky ways of worshiping the Lord that can be downright embarrassing. What kind of example is that for the rest of the world to see? That just gives people who don't understand the culture another stereotype to pin on Black people. Haven't we progressed farther than that?

Obviously not, because Madea shows us that, behind the fancy dresses and big hats are people with some serious life problems. Tyler Perry just tapped a big needle into the "saved, sanctified… and still need a drink" cultural vein, and drew out millions. It was about time somebody called it out. Why not him?

I get it. I was raised in it. I understand it. And if you were raised in that culture, you get it, too! No, you don't really smoke, drink, and beat your kids, but, sometimes, if the Lord doesn't intervene, you are just a prayer away from losing your salvation, which means the feelings are still there and you need to express them, preferably "nonviolently"! If no one else understands, God knows. You may be saved and sanctified, but you are human, and, no, you may not drink, but the thought of a stiff martini does cross your mind in the heat of the moment! A good punch or slap in the mouth may feel more satisfying to unleash on a bratty kid, but it's not appropriate for a Child of the King who has been Born Again.

But where did it all come from? If we are "saved and sanctified," why can't we all do like Madea and have it both ways? Why is it hard for us to say it out loud?

I'm saved, sanctified…and still need a drink!

Saved, Sanctified and Still Need a Drink!

We just can't do it. That's why Madea is so popular. She is our guilty pleasure. She does it for us! I wrote this book because I think it is not only OK to say it—but to embrace it!

INTRODUCTION

Believe it or not, I got my idea for writing this book when I looked at a lot of my own issues and, in especially difficult and confusing situations, asked the question, "What Would Jesus Do?" Instead of visualizing a serious prayer meeting, I conjured up this really funny image of Jesus staging a reality series called "Saved, Sanctified... and **Still** Need a Drink!" Every contestant would be invited to the Cocktail Hour Before The Last Supper. He would have so much fun watching us from the Upper Room. Hidden cameras and instant replays with the best cuts would be posted on Heavenly YouTube® ready for all the angels to check out. There would be no judges, though. Only lessons to learn.

What I really enjoyed imagining though...was *Jesus with a drink!* After all, He's the one that turned water into wine, so why wouldn't He appreciate a glass of Merlot with His serving of two fishes and five loaves of bread?

As I wrote this book, I related to something about Jesus that I truly admired. Jesus *loved to teach*. On this imagined reality show,

I could see Him rolling the cameras on our behaviors as we acted out our dramas, insecurities, and false perceptions. Then Jesus would make us face ourselves, and He would gently lead us to the truth. Can you relate? I hope so!

Now, you may be wondering, who am I to even be writing such a book as this? I am not a preacher, missionary, prophetess, or church mother. I'm not even a Sunday School teacher. I don't have any kind of church position, and no one has given me a special anointing, license, or credential to post on my resume.

I consider myself to be a Wisdom Woman (a title I made up for myself because it's what I wanted to be called after I turned fifty!). My mission is to be a catalyst for others who are seeking personal peace. In order for me to achieve my own sense of personal peace, I practice self-reflection every day, mostly through journaling, prayer, and meditation. I also make sure to do what I love.

As a coach and mentor, I support people who need a safe place to open up and do self-discovery work. I have a calmness about me that is comforting and safe, and most people in my presence say I exude an energy of trust and confidence. That is my spiritual gift. So, even though you don't know me, I invite you to just relax and go with the flow!

Now, it's time for me to explain the basics...

Saved and Sanctified...What Does that Really Mean?

If you are a Christian, then you already know the general doctrine of Christianity, which states that God is the Father, Jesus Christ is His Son, and the Holy Ghost is His Spirit, all the same entity, but with different functions. This doctrine is commonly understood by all Christians, regardless of denomination or sect. Catholics, Lutherans, Baptists, Episcopalians, are some of the major Christian denominations. You may know of others.

Introduction

I grew up in the Church of God In Christ, a predominantly African-American Pentecostal denomination, with millions of members worldwide. It is also known as the "holiness" church. For many years, people who went to holiness churches were referred to as "sanctified folks" or "holy rollers."

"Saved, sanctified, and filled with the Holy Ghost" is a unique statement commonly understood in holiness churches. These words mean something very powerful, like marriage vows. The person knows exactly the commitment they have made to God and are proud to declare it.

When you claim that you are a believer in Jesus Christ, then you believe in the sacrifice that Jesus made when He was crucified for the sins of man. You believe that, through His death, any person who believes in Him is "SAVED."

The "SANCTIFIED" part of the statement means that, as a believer, you are dedicated to cleansing yourself—body, mind, and spirit—to reflect the "new person" who has been "born again."

The "FILLED WITH THE HOLY GHOST" part means that the believer accepts this special spiritual presence, also known as the HOLY SPIRIT, which is the guide that lives inside each person to help them navigate life under God's will.

I want to make it clear that I take this seriously and am in no way making light of this spiritual legacy. So, if any of you think I don't know what it means, I just want to assure you that I do. Why do I stress this? Because I know some of you are still tripping on the title of this book. I can feel it. That's OK.

But guess what? I am a preacher's daughter. I grew up in a family where my maternal grandmother was saved under Bishop C.H. Mason, the founder of the Church of God in Christ, back in the early 1900s. She raised all of her eight children to be in the church and did not believe there was any other religion more valid than hers. My father was a leader in the church. He was the model for how I interpreted all of the teachings and beliefs about the church, about God, and Jesus, and about the Bible. My father studied the Bible, quoted scriptures, preached with anointing and authority, and was widely respected for his no-nonsense approach to all things sacred. He did not play when it came to God.

I was fortunate to receive an excellent academic education. I had a long and productive career as a public health professional, which gave me the opportunity to interact with people from different backgrounds and cultures. My parents were able to keep my siblings and me grounded in the church, to value the spiritual teachings, and to apply them to life in general, although we were also exposed to higher learning, science, and secular beliefs as well.

I am a product of the culture that I grew up in. I know all the nuances, the sayings, and "implied language" of my church. You will find that, in this book, I refer to "testimony service," "shouting," "speaking in tongues," "altar calls," "backsliding," and specific sayings such as "Loose Here Satan, the Lord Rebuke You" as language specific to the Church of God In Christ culture and other holiness brands.

Given my background, I bring to this book a perspective that is all mine. So much has changed in the world of religion and spirituality since I was a child. I've seen growth, and I've seen setbacks. Now that I am officially a Wisdom Woman, I desire to help others who feel stuck in guilt and condemnation get out of the mindset that keeps them from feeling peaceful and content. Religious beliefs can cause those feelings, because they did for me! What better way to help others than by telling my own story? I'm just calling it like I see it.

For me, this book is a cool way to express my self-discovery journey. If I had successfully completed Jesus's reality show, and

Introduction

he asked me, "What did you learn?" I would say that I learned a lot about myself that I did not appreciate before I went through the experience. Thank you, Lord!

So, in setting you up for reading this book, I request only three things:

- I ask you to relate to my examples in your own way and apply them to your own experiences.

- I ask you to keep an open heart, receive what comes to you and through you, and pay attention to what resonates inside of you rather than try to point fingers or judge others.

- I ask that you use this book to talk about the issues, and, if they are of concern, to seek others whom you trust to have a conversation or discussion.

Are you ready? Let's begin...

Chapter 1
WHITE ZINFANDEL

Imagine this scenario. You are shopping at the grocery store, and who do you see? Somebody you know. She is a colleague of yours from your job. She's in the beer and wine aisle. So you wave at her to let her know you see her, but she acts like she doesn't see you. You walk around the store for a minute, thinking you will run into her in another aisle. But you never do, until you finish your shopping and get in the checkout line, right behind her. You know she sees you now, but she is acting really strange.

You happen to glance in her shopping cart, and you spot a bottle of wine. White Zinfandel. As she takes each item out of her cart, her face turns red. Now you get it. She was trying to avoid you. Why?

Because at work, she is known as the "holy roller." She goes to church each and every Sunday, on time, with her Bible and tambourine, ready for a high time in the Lord. If you were to invite her out to Happy Hour after work, she wouldn't think of going. So why is she buying alcohol? You don't even have to ask.

If you are from the "saved and sanctified" church culture, you know what happens next.

You speak to your colleague. All you do is say, "Hello." Instead of saying "Hello" back, she makes an excuse about the alcohol, such as:

"I'm buying this for my husband. He's not saved, you know."

"My son is going to a party, and I was on my way to the store. I didn't want to buy this alcohol, because I just knew I would run into somebody who would see me and think that I was a drinker. He's not saved, but I am working on him!"

"I know this isn't right, so don't tell anyone you saw me here at the store with this alcohol in my cart! I feel so condemned! If you see me at the altar on Sunday, you know why!"

As she slinks out of the store with her bags, you see her almost running to the car. You don't know of any man who drinks White Zinfandel. You just wonder if this is a one-time coincidence or if she just got caught today. It doesn't matter. Somebody in that house needs a drink!

In this scenario, there is the nagging fear of "getting caught" and "feeling guilty." The word used in the "saved and sanctified" culture is **condemnation**. There is a scripture that implies, "If you feel condemned, then God is greater." This is a huge issue for a lot of us coming from the holiness church background.

If I believed I was doing something I had been told was wrong or was a sin, then I felt guilty—especially if I got caught in the act by someone I thought would judge me. I'd feel very ashamed and beat myself up. It would nag me all week long. I just knew on Sunday morning I would feel the need to go to the altar to repent so God would forgive me for trying to sneak and buy that White Zinfandel!

The "drink in the cart" scenario is about getting caught in the open and trying to justify a decision. The wrong, sneaky, and mortifying feelings are real. If you grew up in the church, you may relate to other guilt trips inside yourself that you may not want to admit out loud. Or you have issues that give you that "need a drink" feeling. For example:

- You may secretly wrestle with underlying feelings of guilt about going outside of your church's teachings. You read your Bible, but you also have a copy of "A Course in Miracles" on your nightstand and stay home to watch Eckhart Tolle on Oprah's *Super Soul Sunday®* with a mimosa, when you should be in Sunday School. What drives your guilty feelings? You're not in Sunday School? You're drinking a mimosa? You're reading something other than the Bible to get spiritual information? What would your pastor say if he knew you were a "Super Souler?"

- You struggle with "training up your child in the way he/she should go" when you know that you strayed from the training that you were taught as a child. You fear admitting that you were not a perfect saint and did some things under the table. Your kids or family members would be shocked to find out that you really did have a drink! Or smoked a cigarette! Or tried some "medical marijuana"!

+ You still think that you've disappointed yourself, God, Jesus, your parents, and the church because you backslid, but yet you love the Lord, and no one understands how you feel. You carry a lot of guilt because of something you did, someone you betrayed, or something you lied about.

+ You are tired of judgmental messages that don't make sense to you, and it just doesn't feel good to say you're "saved and sanctified" when you see so much mess in the church. The main ones who are shouting, preaching, testifying, and saying they are so saved seem to be the worst devils. But they get away with it. That's just not right.

+ You are tired of the misuse of the Word of God and people saying things because they believe it's what "the Bible says," but couldn't find the scripture in the Dead Sea Scrolls, let alone any variation of the Bible that is out there today.

+ You spend a lot of your energy bemoaning the state of the church, complaining that these "unseasoned pastors" and "untrained members" don't know what "'saved and sanctified" really represents, because they let anyone and everyone come in and do whatever they want. What happened to the standards? Where's the *"Come out of the world and be ye separate"* part of holiness?

+ You feel that "saved and sanctified" is too commercialized and made to be comical and funny. You are concerned about the image of the Black church being tied to *Madea Goes to Jail*. Isn't it important to represent your faith in a way that others take you seriously? When visitors come to your church who don't understand your quirky members, you feel embarrassed and ashamed that "Brother Roscoe" will pick that Sunday to act a fool. That just plays into the stereotypes.

✦ You are confused, ashamed, or indifferent as to what your church's history represents in your life. You grew up with it, the rest of your family is still in it, but you don't want to claim it for yourself. You feel like you've disappointed your family, but you still crave their acceptance, even though you don't claim to be saved and sanctified.

Now does it resonate? Well, guess what? I understand how you feel, and I want you to know I've dealt with all of these issues at some point in my life. This is the time to explore what is behind the concerns you may have. Because we are all in this together!

Chapter 2
BLOODY MARY OR SHIRLEY TEMPLE?

Let's just take a minute and address it right now. I don't know about you, but every perception of what is "sinful" and "wrong" is appropriate for examination as to how it pertains to being "saved and sanctified." So let's go there!

For each question, answer according to your first impression. Don't think about it. Just check one of three boxes: Yes, No, or Not Sure.

Note: I know some of you distinguish a big difference between "saved," "sanctified," and "filled with the Holy Ghost." Assume that it's all the same for this exercise. Just go with your gut feeling.

Saved, Sanctified and Still Need a Drink!

Can You Be Saved and Sanctified and Still:

	YES	NO	NOT SURE
Smoke cigarettes			
Smoke weed (marijuana)			
Drink alcohol			
Have sex out of wedlock			
Be gay, lesbian, bisexual, or transgendered			
Get a divorce and remarry			
Go to the movies or to live concerts			
Go to a nightclub and party with friends			
Date or marry somebody who is not saved and sanctified			
Wear pants (women)			
Wear pants to church (women)			
Wear makeup (lipstick, eyeshadow, etc.)			
Get piercings and tattoos on your body			
Curse or say a "bad word" sometimes			
Use birth control, married or not			
Have an abortion, married or not			
Own a gun			
Carry a pistol			
Listen to rap and hip-hop music			
Whip your children			
Hit your husband or wife			
Gossip behind someone's back			

Go to war			
Give up your baby for adoption			
Have kinky sex			
Not pay your tithes			
Not go to church regularly or at all			
Be in the entertainment industry as a singer, actor, dancer, or comedian			
Go to strip clubs			
Read erotica or watch porn or a sex tape			
Have an affair or be unfaithful			
Use crack, cocaine, heroin, or meth			
Take pain pills and prescription drugs even when you don't need them for pain			
Live an extravagant lifestyle with lots of material things to show for it			

Now answer these questions as truthfully and honestly as possible… don't hold back!

What came up for you overall when you first looked at the questionnaire? What was your first impression? What did you feel?

Saved, Sanctified and Still Need a Drink!

As you checked the boxes, did any of the behaviors feel more "sinful" to you than others? Which ones? Why?

Based on what you believe it requires for you to say you're saved and sanctified, how do you make sense of what is right or wrong to do?

What behaviors (if any) make you feel "guilty" or "condemned" if somebody saw you doing them?

Chapter 3
THE CONFESSION BAR

If you are like me, you may "need a drink" about now, just to process within yourself what you are thinking and feeling. That's OK! This is about you and nobody else but you!

I went through the questionnaire, surprised at what my answers revealed for me. I realized that my image of what being saved and sanctified meant was based on how I was raised. My answers were not congruent at all with what I had been taught.

The standards that I used to measure myself were pretty high. I said NO to a lot of the questions, and those values really informed my beliefs about whether I was "qualified" to be saved and sanctified. Depending on your religious upbringing, you may have very different ideas. That is why I did not assign a score to each issue. Who am I to judge?

I love the Church of God in Christ. I love my history. I admire the saints who can get up and shout the victory and testify that they are saved and sanctified, and testify to what the Lord has brought them through. In my mind, I can't imagine "Missionary Brown" leaving church and going home smoking or drinking or "Deacon Jones" beating his wife. I can't picture "Elder Smith" at the clubs or casinos or running into him and his Sunshine Band Leader daughter at the Beyonce concert. I don't see any of the saints having affairs or lying, cheating, or stealing. I see halos around their heads. I just don't have one around mine, and I am still afraid that when I go to church, others will notice. When altar-call time comes, all heads turn in my direction. But I just sit in my seat, bow my head, and wait it out.

Because I know that when I go home, I may pull out a bottle of wine and drink some. I will slip and use some profanity. Not often, but every now and then. I will go to the nightclub on Saturday night, although I'm not a barfly. Since I still feel a twinge of guilt, I don't wear tight jeans and low-cut tops and super high heels and tons of makeup.

I don't like rap and hip-hop that talks about women as "bitches and hos," but I could get with some of the rappers who are controversial in the church. I don't like a lot of violent movies, but my guilty pleasure is to partake in the blood and gore of certain cult classics that I know are just designed to be entertainment. The ID (Investigation Discovery) channel keeps me intrigued with shows like *Who the Bleep Did I Marry?* and *Deadly Women* more than the Family Channel, or *Glee* and *The Golden Girls*. I have no desire to murder anyone, but I love *Forensic Files* because of the science of finding crooks and criminals that lies in the DNA profiles, and I want to see how they get caught and brought to justice.

I go to different churches, but I don't belong to any of them. I just like to hear the message, listen to good singing, and feel the collective spirit of the saints in worship. I don't like the politics, the money begging, and the judgmental insinuations that I encounter, so when I see that is what's going on, I politely tip out.

Besides that, I've been married three times, and all my husbands are **still alive**. Not like my grandmother, who made it clear that she was married three times, but her husbands **died** before she remarried. Big difference!

I even owned and operated a nightclub as a business venture. To keep it going, I tried different angles to get the right crowd to support the business. Swingers, hip-hop, jazz, salsa, "fat girlz" and even gay with drag queens and everything—and I'm not gay. What is a saved and sanctified woman doing owning any nightclub? Long story! But I had some saved and sanctified church people come by and check it out. Probably because I was the owner, and that made it more acceptable. Who knows?

The one and only time I got pregnant was a disaster. It was an ectopic (tubal) pregnancy, so my baby had to be aborted. Medical emergency, I was told. My doctor said I could die if it wasn't removed. But although I was a public health professional and well-educated about the situation, it didn't matter when I heard some of the saints judging me because if had I just allowed the pregnancy to continue and trusted God, then God would have worked a miracle, and I could have had a healthy baby, despite the odds. I didn't take the risk, but I did feel a twinge of guilt that my faith wasn't strong enough.

Despite my father's hatred of the sin of gambling, I do go to Las Vegas and Reno now. I even play Powerball and Megabucks sometimes. I even go to the casinos and boats on the Indian reservations. I may gamble $20 on the slot machines, but I take my money out as soon as I win. However, I still haven't learned how to play cards (except Solitaire on my cell phone app) or dice or dominoes. You won't see me at a bid whist or poker tournament.

Even though it may be OK to wear pants to church, I still show respect and put on a dress. But maybe not wear pantyhose, because I live in Arizona, and it's just too hot. I also feel uncomfortable if I wear too much bling or glitz. It just seems inappropriate to me.

I have smoked cigarettes off and on during my life. Mostly because I was mad about something. I remember the first time I smoked. I was angry, and I had never considered smoking a cigarette before. But I happened to go to the Ebony Fashion Fair, and they used to put a free pack of More cigarettes on everyone's chair (remember those?). I picked up a pack and decided to try smoking one. I felt guilty, but I didn't care. I wanted to show I was angry.

Of course, I could go on and on with other things I've done and felt condemned about. Did you feel the need to judge me, now that I've come clean? I hope that you looked at my confession and related to it, because that is what I want you to do as well. Relax! Don't beat yourself up so much. It will all make sense to you as you live your own life. The first step to healing is to "confess"…which just means to admit openly and tell the truth!

I feel better already! And you will, too, once you tell your story! And guess what? Your worst fear will be conquered! Then you can move on.

Why is it so important to tell the truth? First of all, it is freeing. It allows you to be honest. And it makes sense to give voice to your own behavior.

I found it so freeing when I admitted my "stuff" and felt the guilt, the fear, and the perceived rejection, punishment, and condemnation. I then saw what was causing the pain. I could feel where my energy was going. I could touch the places in my body where I felt nervousness, headaches, nausea, anxiety, stress, and worry. I could identify with all of it.

Chapter 4

OLD FASHIONED OR NEW SCHOOL?

Take a few minutes now to go back to the questionnaire and review your answers again.

For those of you who answered all or most of the questions with a YES, I say your "go to" scriptures may be from the New Testament Gospels, where Jesus was featured prominently saying things like: "Judge not that ye be not judged," or "He who has not sinned, let him cast the first stone," or "All have sinned and come short of the glory of God."

You like the way Jesus handled the Scribes and Pharisees, the woman at the well, and the prostitute who washed Jesus's feet. He just loved all the sinners and wretches undone. It didn't matter how wrong others saw you, in Jesus's eyes, you were saved, as long as

Saved, Sanctified and Still Need a Drink!

you just believed in Him. Just like the thief hanging next to Jesus on the cross at Calvary.

But is it that easy? Are there some values that, as a Christian, you just hold because you feel you have to represent yourself as a witness? If you are into strippers and pornography, is that going too far, or does it even matter?

For those of you who answered all or most of the questions with a NO, you have your favorite set of scriptures to address your beliefs, too. They come either from select passages in the Old Testament, where God was strict and punitive to the disobedient Jews, or from those that the Apostle Paul wrote in the New Testament epistles, because before he was Paul, he was Saul. He had an alter ego. The new "born again, saved and sanctified" Paul hated the old "sinful, evil, Christian-persecuting" Saul. So when he converted to Christianity, he just didn't play with sinful behavior, and when he wrote his letters to the Romans, the Ephesians, and the other churches, he got his points across beautifully.

If you profess to be **"saved and sanctified, and filled with the Holy Ghost"** according to Acts 2:4, then you are transformed from head to toe, and everyone knows it. The things you used to do, you don't do any more. You became a new creature, and all the desire to be sinful and worldly magically disappeared. How can you call yourself saved and sanctified and still go to the nightclubs, the strip clubs, the gambling halls, and the movies and concerts? How could you be saved and sanctified and beat your wife or cuss out your boss? You shouldn't have any desire to go do anything that is out of line.

Pick your favorite scripture to justify why you can't be saved if you do this, that, or the other. Some of you have them all memorized and wield them just like a two-edged sword. Madea included.

But is it that easy? If you are so strict and dogmatic that everything you think is a sin means you can't be saved and sanctified

Old Fashioned or New School?

if you do them, then are you at risk of being judgmental toward others who do? Are you so rigid and inflexible in your beliefs that you come across as belonging to a cult?

Many of you may have a mixture of YES, NO, **and** NOT SURE. That just means you don't see things all one way. There may be some caveats. You may read the Bible differently and have a perspective that is more contemporary. After all, the Bible was put together thousands of years ago. This is now.

Some things are not the same, and it's OK now. Like women wearing pants to church or wearing makeup. Nobody's trying to be Jezebel these days. Whoever she was. And not every woman is a "virtuous" woman, either. So you don't have to hear Proverbs 31:10–31 every Women's Day any more. We women can preach and teach just like the men. And have sex with the lights on with our sexy lingerie, as long as it's with our husbands.

But is it that easy? Which areas are you still struggling with? Where do you feel a twinge of guilt? How do you know? What if you never get the answer? Can you still make a decision that you feel comfortable with? Can you communicate your behavior and your choices to your children? Can you still feel you are acting with integrity?

Well, if you are comfortable doing this, I want you to work through your own feelings, and come up with *your own answers*. There is no right or wrong here, so even if you feel like there is, or should be, don't put that on yourself. Just see what comes up for you first, and then feel free to use the questionnaire and the scenarios I presented as a way to bring up the conversation.

Then, if you dare, discuss amongst yourselves and your family and even with your other friends, whether or not they are saved and sanctified. I also ask those of you who are saved and sanctified to challenge your thinking. What drives your beliefs? Is it what you've been taught? What you heard someone else say? What makes sense or doesn't make sense to you? What you've personally experienced? What the Bible says? What the pastor or missionary told you?

Get it clear. Write down whatever comes up for you. It matters. This may be a good time to grab a seat and have a drink (of your choice!) by your side, so you can relax and just allow the answers and insights to reveal themselves. I'm still with you! Just take a deep breath, and let it all go!

A lot of your struggles with these questions may be related to confusion between what you have been taught because of history and tradition, as opposed to what is verified by a religious figure whom you respect and revere, versus what can be backed by a passage in the Bible.

Maybe you just don't know what is right or wrong or who to believe anymore. Maybe you feel that it just doesn't matter. Which makes your own opinion and feelings that much more important to recognize. Do you know how *you feel* and what *you think* and what *you believe*? If not, don't you think you should?

Chapter 5
"TOP SHELF" OR "OFF BRAND"

Imagine this scenario. Your friend's grandmother is in town for the weekend. She wants to take her grandmother to church on Sunday but isn't sure where to take her. You ask your friend what denomination her grandmother belongs to. She says "holiness church." "Does that mean she is "saved and sanctified?" you ask. "Not only that, but filled with the Holy Ghost and *that with fire!*" You and your friend laugh.

That's all you need to know. You look up a few churches in the directory and find one that looks good. The pastor and his wife are posing together in a glossy photo ad for their church. They look young, but definitely saved and sanctified. You call your friend and tell her about the church, and she agrees to check it out. You even decide to go to church with them, since you haven't stepped foot in a real holiness church in many years.

Saved, Sanctified and Still Need a Drink!

On Sunday, you get prepared. You want to make sure you are dressed modestly, knowing how particular the holiness churches are about these things. You put on your long dress, dig out your panty hose, take out your nose ring, cover up your tattoos with a long-sleeved sweater, and make sure your makeup is simple and clean. You dust off your Bible and make sure your cleavage is covered up.

When you see your friend's grandmother, you know you are in the presence of a saint. Grandma is decked out in her three-piece white suit, with a beautiful matching hat, and a white lace handkerchief in her hand, ready to drape on her lap as soon as she sits down in the front-row pew with all the other church mothers. After all, this is the fifth Sunday. Women's day, of course!

So, imagine your surprise and shock when you walk into the church, and it looks like a pep rally! All the women are wearing pants. Jeans, even! The music sounds like a hip-hop concert. The young people are dancing like they do at the nightclub. And there is so much cleavage and booty showing. You think you've walked onto the set of a rap video! Grandma is scowling. You know what she is thinking.

"I don't know what this is, but it's not holiness! This is some "off brand" church! This is not how 'saved and sanctified' is supposed to look!"

She endures the hip-hop praise and dance-team routine, but when Grandma sees the pastor's wife get up behind the pulpit in her pink pantsuit to bring the message, that does it. Rolling her eyes, she's ready to go.

You whisper to your friend, "Girl, we need a drink!" She replies, laughing so hard, "No, we don't…but Grandma does!"

· · · · · ·

In this scenario, Grandma is upset because she is used to seeing a certain protocol in the holiness church that was not evident in the church she visited. It would be like going to McDonald's expecting to get a Big Mac, and instead, getting something like a "happy hour special" at Joe's Social Club! That's why she called it "off brand."

Holiness churches do have brand names. Ours was the Church of God in Christ. Our brand had a specific protocol. No matter how long you may have been out of the church, when it's time to go to a service, you know what to expect and how to act.

You don't come into church wearing any old kind of thing. You dress appropriately.

You know the order of service. It opens with prayer. There is time in the program for testimony service, praise and worship, an A and B selection from the choir, offering time, where you get up and walk to the table to put your money in the basket or your tithes in the envelope.

Then the church secretary reads the announcements. The choir comes back with a C selection before the pastor gets up to preach the sermon. After the sermon, it is time for the altar call. Anyone who wants to get saved is invited to come up front, and the prayer warriors come around and pray with them. Before service is dismissed, there are last-minute words from any visiting dignitaries. The entire service runs about two hours. That's not including Sunday School.

It is the tradition of **testimony service** that those of us who have been raised in the Church of God in Christ can distinguish who is proud to be "saved and sanctified" because they will tell you upfront. Everyone who stands up to give their personal testimony *always* begins with the statement **"Giving Honor to God..."**; then they give honor to a host of others. The pattern is hierarchical, from top to bottom. From the pastor, pastor's wife, ministers, saints, and friends.

The next part of the testimony is a statement of one's status. "I thank the Lord for being **saved, sanctified,** and **filled with the**

Holy Ghost." This is also hierarchical. "Saved" is always first. "Sanctified" is always second. "Filled with the Holy Ghost" is always last. That way you can know where the person stands. They may be saved only. Or they may be "saved and sanctified" but "not yet filled." If they had all three, then they were all in!

Then the testimony would be about whatever the person wanted to share with the congregation.

"The Lord saved me from a life of sin and shame."

"I woke up this morning with my mind stayed on Jesus."

"He didn't have to do it, but He did."

Plus, so many people will use this opportunity to share what happened during the week, what they were grateful and thankful for, and what particular blessing or miracle they experienced that they could attribute to God's intervention in their lives. The testimony usually ends with *"Please pray my strength in the Lord!"*

When everyone in the congregation blends together with the spirit of the service, it is an amazing, beautiful, spiritual presence that shows up. Everyone is in "one accord." The old and the young. The saved and the unsaved. When everything is right—the music, the powerful testimony from one of the saints, the praise and worship expressions, the moving of the Holy Spirit in the room—it is electric. Sacred. Powerful enough to change lives. To make people want to give their lives to God. To drive souls to the altar to get saved!

But when things are "off," like the music is too loud, or the singing is not appropriate for the occasion, or the person giving the message is saying things that are not "scriptural," or the people who testify use the space to be critical and "throw shade" at somebody else, and you come out of the service feeling worse than when you went in, there is something wrong.

"Top Shelf" or "Off Brand"

Grandma didn't feel uplifted at the "off brand" church. She felt like Jesus when He went into the temple and tossed tables and chairs around because He saw what the moneychangers had done. That's why her granddaughter laughed and said she "needed a drink."

I get why Grandma felt disturbed, because she saw the history and traditions of the church were not being upheld. Somewhere along the way, people stopped passing down the values of the holiness way of life. There used to be something "different" and "peculiar" about the saints, and now there was no distinction from those who are "in the church" from those who are "out of the church." Believe me—there used to be a difference!

Chapter 6
THIS ONE'S "ON THE HOUSE"

"*Kids, I am tired of you running in and out of this house! So you need to make a decision! Either you are going to stay inside, or you're going to stay outdoors. What's it going to be?*"

We all know what that means, right?

Outside. It's fun out there. Our friends are calling us to come out and play. We want to keep rolling in the grass and kicking the soccer ball. Chase the dogs, and scream and yell at the top of our lungs. We want to be free and be ourselves!

Inside. It's quiet in there. We have to sit down and be still. We have to do our homework, eat dinner, use the bathroom. Stay out of the way of the grownups. Go into our rooms. Get cleaned up and wash our faces and hands. Take off our dirty clothes. Wash the dishes.

Why can't we just do both? Go outside and play a while and then come inside and cool off, get some food and water, or a popsicle, and go back outside again?

That's because the adults need the door shut. When we go back and forth through the door, we bring in stuff. Flies, mosquitos, mud. Those are not wanted inside. Flies and mosquitos buzz and bite. Mud dirties up the carpet. The dog can't come inside, because he might bring in fleas. Fleas are a nuisance. Our friends can't come inside. Who are their parents? Do we know these people coming in and out of our house?

Opening and closing the door also changes the house temperature. Inside it may be cool. Outside, it may be hot. They can't keep changing the thermostat. That costs energy.

The door needs to stay shut after the adults are tired of the noise we kids make. They don't want to have to keep telling us over and over. So, if we don't have sense enough to know when to come into the house, then that is when they frame it as a choice we have to make.

> *"I'm only going to say this one more time! Come in, or stay out. What's your decision?"*

I use this analogy to explain the mindset of people who were in the holiness movement at the time my father was converted to Christianity.

The year was 1960. I was seven years old. I remember it like it was yesterday. My father got saved, sanctified, and filled with the Holy Ghost in the Church of God in Christ. He was thirty years old and had been a gambler and street hustler in Oakland, California. He was on the brink of a meltdown, about to destroy his family with his gambling addiction, and my mother was ready to commit suicide, with me and my brother in tow. But God intervened and saved him.

His conversion was like the Apostle Paul in the book of Acts. While he was leaving the gambling hall, flat broke and in a state of despair because he had gambled up all of his paycheck and knew he couldn't face my mother, all of a sudden, he heard God's voice, as plain as day, say to him, "If you go back, I will kill you!"

Frightened and shaken, he didn't go back to the gambling hall, but he bee-lined straight to the first church he could find that was open at midnight. The pastor of that church opened the door, prayed with him, told him to go back home to his wife and kids, and explained to him that if God called him out of sin, then he couldn't go back into "the world." **Ever!** If he did, he would die. That night, my father turned from street-hustler/gambler to born-again Christian and evangelist for the Lord. Just like Paul.

My mother was so happy and relieved that God jumped in and saved her husband. Nobody else had gotten through to him, but this transformation was sudden and unmistakable. He was different. He stopped smoking, drinking, gambling, and turned his life over to Christ. Forever.

What did that mean for us? After his life-altering experience, our whole household changed. I didn't know what it meant to be saved, but I soon found out. I had to go to church more. I couldn't go roller skating with my dad anymore. He wasn't any fun. All he did was pray and hang out with other preachers. Things got real strict, and he was more judgmental. God saved him, not me. But because he was my father, whatever he was saved from, I was saved from.

The first Bible scripture I remember him talking about to explain why we couldn't do the things we used to do was from the New Testament. It said:

> *"Wherefore come out from among them, and be ye separate, saith the Lord, and touch not the unclean thing; and I will receive you, and will be a Father unto you, and ye shall be my sons and daughters, saith the Lord Almighty."*
> — II CORINTHIANS 6:17–18

When my father got saved, God told him, in essence, to quit running in and out of the house. Because he was so afraid of what would happen to him if he stayed "outside," he made a clear decision. To come inside. For good.

That meant he wasn't going back out "in the world." He worked hard to get himself cleaned up, by denouncing sin, giving up his wicked ways, stopping the gambling, the smoking, the drinking, and committing his life to the Lord. Once he did the work to clean up his life, he had to keep the door closed, because he did not want to know what God would do to him if he went back outside.

My father needed his door closed. No screen option. No peephole. No looking back. When he closed the door, it was shut. By keeping the door completely shut, there was no way to track in dirt or let in the flies and the mosquitos. He had put the dog out, and he was really afraid that, if he opened the door, the dog would come back in, tracking mud and bringing in fleas.

So, because of his decision, it was a done deal. Nobody in the house could open the door. We all had to stay inside.

This One's "On the House"

The Bible verse that he quoted to make sure we understood that this was non-negotiable was from the Old Testament:

> *"And if it seem evil unto you to serve the* LORD, *choose you this day whom ye will serve; whether the gods which your fathers served that were on the other side of the flood, or the gods of the Amorites, in whose land ye dwell: but as for me and my house, we will serve the* LORD.
> — JOSHUA 24:15

Chapter 7
STRAIGHT, NO CHASER

All of a sudden, I became a preacher's kid. Back in the 1960s and '70s, when I grew up, the Church of God in Christ (C.O.G.I.C.) was all about "holiness or hell." Holiness churches then were known for being strict and rigid. Everything was pretty black and white. Cut and dried. The C.O.G.I.C. motto was **"You can't JOIN in, You've got to be BORN in!"** It wasn't like the churches are today, where you come on Sunday, enjoy the service, decide this will be your church home, sign the membership book, and start paying your tithes and offerings. Back then, just being a member did not mean you were saved. You had some work to do. Like my father did.

Just like learning a new language, it took a few years for me to get it. If you have been immersed in the "holiness" church culture

Saved, Sanctified and Still Need a Drink!

for any length of time, you may recognize some of the "code speak" for what I call "IN HERE" and "OUT THERE."

"IN HERE"	"OUT THERE"
"You are saved!"	"You are NOT saved!"
Saved, sanctified, and filled with the Holy Ghost—proud to testify in church. Sing and shout the victory!	Working up to the day when you can testify in church that you are "SSandFwith the HG!" Until then, keep quiet and pray.
You live right! All day, all night, all the time!	You live in sin! Whatever that means! It's all evil!
The holiness church, with all its blessings and Godly favors	The "world", with all its temptations, trials, and tribulations!
Come back and repent. Try it again. This time, get it right!	Stay gone until you are ready to come back in. This is not a game! It's heaven or hell!
God loves you...	But He hates your evil ways!
You love the Lord!	The Devil is busy!
Heaven is a holy place!	Hell is fire and brimstone!

Since we couldn't just "JOIN in" and had to be "BORN in," it was always an issue. Each Sunday we went to church, we had to make a decision. What's it going to be? Inside or outside? Holiness or hell?

Using the language of "IN HERE" and "OUT THERE," this is how I interpreted what it meant to "be BORN in."

If I die, I want go to heaven. If I want to go to heaven, I have to "get saved." If I get "saved," I have to "live right." I can't "live right" unless I get "sanctified." That means "shutting the door to the outside." I can't stay "sanctified" unless I have "the Holy Ghost." That means I have to ask God to "fill me with the Holy

Ghost." I would have to be ready to "tarry," "shout the victory," and "speak in tongues." I would then have the power to resist "temptation" and "command the Devil to flee far from me." That way, I would be able to live a life "free from sin," so whenever I die, or when Jesus comes back (whichever comes first), I can go to heaven and not go to hell. If I don't want to go to hell, I better decide to get right with the Lord. Because tomorrow is not promised to me, and it may be too late! Is this the Sunday to do it? Or can I wait a little longer, when I know I am ready to finally come inside and shut the door to the world of sin and shame?

So every altar call, I cringed. Why? No matter how the invitation to come up to the altar was offered, what I heard and felt was:

*"I'm only going to say this one more time!
Come in, or stay out. What's your decision?"*

"Strong" or "Watered Down"?

As a young child growing up in the church, the decision to "come in" or "stay out" felt like a huge weight on my shoulders. It was like making a decision to get married or something. Once married, no divorce! When I was introduced to the *rules* of this new "saved and sanctified" lifestyle, it felt to me like the door was not only shut to the outside world, but it was padlocked, chained, and double-bolted!

Back in the 1960s and '70s, the holiness churches had behavioral rules that were quite specific. Being a teenager, I had a lot of conflict with rules that said if I was going to be "saved," I couldn't wear the latest fashions, such as:

- ✦ Big Angela Davis style Afros *(too extreme, rebellious, militant)*

- Mini skirts or hot pants *(showing too much leg or skin)*
- Maxi skirts *(one would think that would be OK, but the length was too extreme)*
- Makeup, fingernail polish, bare shoulders *(no Michelle Obama sleeveless dresses)*, or sandals with the heels out.
- Bright, flashy colors, especially the color red *(that was the color of the harlot Jezebel in the Old Testament)*

I also found that I couldn't engage in "worldly" activities, such as:
- Go to the movies, listen to dance music or any music other than gospel
- Go to any parties or dances *(forget about going to the prom!)*
- Drink, smoke, or take any drugs *(those were just understood as sinful behaviors, Bible scripture or not)*
- Wear pants *(women should not wear male apparel—that famous scripture in Deuteronomy!)*
- Cursing or using any kind of profanity—and if you slipped up and said "Hell" or "Damn," you needed to pray on the spot!

At that time, I used to wonder why God was so strict on us and not on other Christians. Even the Baptists let their members smoke cigarettes in church on the back row. My Catholic friends got to go to the movies and the parties. But for me, being saved and sanctified was hard work. And over the years, it became a real burden, especially being a preacher's daughter.

But, I discovered later that the strict rules of behavior were hard on a lot of people. I'm sure they tried to live a saved and sanctified life, but not everyone could do it. I knew many of them "needed a drink" when there were no answers for them, but guilt and the fear of going to hell was too strong. So either they endured, or, like my one and only brother did, said *"F---it...I'll just go to hell!"* See, I can't even type out the word! Guilty!

I found there were several ways most of us "saved and sanctified" kids of the '60s and '70s era turned out as a result of our upbringing. When we became adults, we either became just as devout and strict in our faith as our parents were or totally rejected everything we were taught to believe. Or we straddled the fence because we knew how to do it. By accepting certain beliefs but rejecting others, we dealt with a lot of our guilt, lies, and fear in all kinds of creative ways. We didn't want to go to hell, but we knew we needed a drink! So we took our chances!

In the 1980s, I continued to struggle with the rules. Some I agreed with, and some I didn't think were relevant at all. Those of us who had our own kids and still wanted them to be raised in church decided to lighten up on them so they wouldn't be rebelling against us later. We took them to church, but we gravitated to the churches that allowed some slack. Over those years, I noticed that even my father was loosening up. The strict rules of holiness or hell began to bend, where:

- Girls could wear pants *(but not too tight!)*
- We could even wear pants to some churches *(very progressive!)*
- We could wear makeup, but not too much. A little powder, blush, and nude lip gloss was fine.
- We didn't feel guilty listening to music that's hip-hop or R&B, as long as it had a "good message."

When I first heard the song "Stomp" by Kirk Franklin and the Family being played by the disc jockey in the nightclub, I felt really condemned! It still didn't feel quite right to want to pop my fingers and dance. But I rationalized it like everyone else...at least it had a good message and was reaching all the unsaved people who would never come to church. Didn't Edwin Hawkins do the same thing in 1968 with "Oh Happy Day"?

I always thought the new "praise dancing" and the hip-hop style rapping in the church was a big change that I couldn't quite get with. I was like the Grandma in my scenario. It seemed out of line to me. But there was Bible scripture that supported it *(technically speaking)*. After all, isn't that what the whole book of Psalms is all about?

Instead of freestyle "shouting," where you could practice your Funky Chicken moves under the guise of being moved by the Spirit, you could now get on the "praise dance" team and do your choreographed pieces with beautiful Christian praise worship music to accompany your compositions.

Another big change was the way churches were raising money. I remember my father spending at least fifteen minutes at the offering table cajoling people to give. Taking up an offering used to be an art form. It took a lot of skill to get people to switch from giving just dimes and nickels to putting some dollar bills in the offering plate.

The new church leaders didn't have to hustle money by begging people for big offerings like in the old days. Instead of selling chicken dinners after service and on Saturday afternoons, these progressive churches were selling DVD's, T-shirts, mugs, tapes, books, and "hot off the press" Sunday sermons to be consumed anytime we were ready to listen or read. They even had raffles! What would be next—bingo?

Although it seemed strange at first, the changes were quite freeing for me. Risky, daring, and definitely out of the box! I loved the idea of going to church wearing slacks or a pantsuit, because I grew up feeling like if I even *thought* about wearing pants, I would go to hell. Even though the pastor still chastised homosexuals and whoremongers, I now felt like the sin of wearing pants was passé.

Mostly, I remember all the years when I had the feeling of "needing a drink" but never acted on it. I mean, I never drank a drop of alcohol in high school. Even in college. I was too afraid. But in the '80s, at the age of twenty-six, I finally felt I could take a sip of wine or drink a beer without going to hell. It was such a relief after I allowed the harsh feeling of guilt to wash over my conscience to find out that nothing had changed. I was still the same. God still loved me. Oh Happy Day!

But I also found myself doing a lot of questioning and struggling with answers. I still had to make sense out of the years of rigid thinking as I transitioned into more open-mindedness. I didn't discover until years later that this was normal to experience.

Chapter 8
A BIG HANGOVER

The reason I think it is so important and healthy to challenge what you think and believe about God based on your history and traditions is that, if you are like me, you discover later on in life that a lot of it has nothing to do with the truth.

> *"Do you remember the year you found out that Santa Claus wasn't real?"*

Maybe it was the year you got up a little too early to go peek under the tree, hoping to catch a glimpse of Santa bringing you the bike you wanted so badly. Instead, you caught your parents pulling the bike out of the attic.

Then you started putting two and two together. How could Santa come down the chimney to put presents under the tree? You didn't have a chimney in your house.

And another thing…how did Santa ride in a sleigh with reindeer when it didn't even snow where you lived?

And by the way, come to think of it—how did Santa really know whether you were naughty or nice? If he really knew the truth, he wouldn't be stopping by your house. Everybody was naughty!

Now it all made sense. Every year when you sat on Santa's lap, he was always white, jolly, and had a fluffy beard. This year, when you went to see Santa and he was Black, you were traumatized! There was no such thing as a Black Santa Claus!

As the truth dawned on you, how did you feel? Betrayed? Deceived? Disappointed? Or did you feel relieved that you weren't crazy? Why didn't somebody just tell you that Santa Claus wasn't for real?

Well…who was going to be the one to burst your bubble? And once you found out the truth, who was going to explain it to you? Who was going to tell you the truth and answer your questions?

Certainly not Santa Claus!

Over the years, as I grew up, went to college, and got exposed to other religions and other cultures, I began to go through my "Santa Claus isn't real" phase when it came to my church and all the things I was taught about God, Jesus, heaven, hell, and the Bible. I was experiencing all the feelings: Betrayal. Disappointment. Anger. And some relief, too. Have you had those moments?

Like when you found out that Jesus wasn't that white, bearded man with the blue eyes and shoulder-length shaggy hair style who wore only one outfit—the long, flowing robe draped so perfectly around his body. And the sandals.

A Big Hangover

Or, were you shocked to even think that Jesus could be depicted as someone of another race! But then, if he came from the Middle East, then who over there looks like "White Jesus?"

What about when Jesus turned water into wine, and you dared asked the question in Sunday School: "Was the wine *really* wine like we drink today?" Did Jesus really make alcohol? And the answer was, "No, it was just grape juice!"

Or, why didn't Jewish people believe that Jesus was the Messiah? What was that about? Wasn't the Bible written by Jews?

How did a virgin have a baby? I really never understood what happened there, and although I put two and two together, it just didn't sit well with me to imagine how it all went down.

Although it didn't make sense, I went with the stories and the explanations that were standard beliefs and traditions. Before, I just had the questions in the back of my mind, and I went along with the program.

But as I got older, went to school, and other kids started asking me questions and challenging what they were told by their parents or their church leaders about God, I began to question some of the things I was taught as well.

Like, why couldn't women preach? Some of the women in my church could "preach" better than the men. Because somewhere in the Bible, it said that only men could preach.

Or, why did God hate gay people? Because somewhere in the Bible it said that men who loved men were an abomination to God. But what about King David and Jonathan? They loved each other, and nobody had a problem with it then.

I started to recognize that my saved and sanctified holiness church culture had a lot of "isms." What we now call racism, sexism, homophobia, and a lot of prejudice against others. The "IN

Saved, Sanctified and Still Need a Drink!

HERE" and "OUT THERE" thinking was rampant and widespread! I didn't realize how deep-seated it was until I began to question things more. Once the floodgates opened, it was like I had just unleashed the contents of Pandora's Box!

I began to match up the messages I had been hearing for years with my questions. Which ones were really true? And which ones didn't make any sense?

It started with the racial questions. We went to an *all-Black* church. No white people ever came to our services. Why not? Was church supposed to be so segregated? If so, then why did our Black church hang huge pictures of White Jesus on the walls? Why did we have to see White Jesus on the back of our church fans donated to us by the Black funeral home in the community? Where were the Black Jesus pictures?

No one ever explained why Jesus always looked like a white man with blue eyes and long hair, the same way that Santa Claus always looked like a white man with a fluffy beard. They were iconic images, steeped in centuries of tradition, and those images always stayed the same, regardless of how times changed. But times did change. During my teen years in the 1970s, when Black Power was at its height, "White Jesus" was an issue!

I had questions about the role of women. Why was it that every fifth Sunday was Women's Day, when there were only a few fifth Sundays in the whole year? Why did women have to stay out of the pulpit? Why did the male leaders get bigger offerings than the female leaders?

I had questions about dressing. Why did they always tell us that "women should dress in modest apparel" and that we couldn't wear nice slacks that drew no attention to us. What about all the big, outrageous hats and gaudy outfits that the saints would wear to the Women's Convention?

I had questions about infidelity, marriage, divorce, babies "out of wedlock," gambling, smoking, drinking, guns, drugs—everything that I thought was supposed to be "OUT THERE." I opened the door and started really looking at what was going on "OUT THERE." The behaviors. The people doing them. Were they all "sinners and wretches undone?" Was that really true? Did that make any sense?

What *would* Jesus do? I really wanted to know! Even more, I wanted someone besides Jesus to talk to. A real human being who didn't use Jesus as the answer for everything. I wanted to be heard and supported as an individual with my own feelings and beliefs. I didn't need the Bible to justify every question. I needed my own intuition. My own voice. Who would listen to me and understand?

Sometimes I thought that, if I told anyone how I was feeling, they would laugh at me. Or dismiss me. Or tell me to pray more. I also was afraid that I wouldn't be able to express my thoughts and be taken seriously. Who wants to debate the Bible? Who wants to question God's Word? I definitely couldn't talk to my father—after all, he was a preacher. Maybe if he weren't, he would see things like I did. What did preachers' kids do when they wanted to talk about stuff that was not religious in nature? What did the "inside" kids do when they wanted to find out how the "outside" world worked for themselves?

I rebelled in my own way. I didn't go crazy, but I guess I tested the waters and put my big toe in it from time to time. But I always came back inside when I felt I wasn't sure, or didn't feel safe. I just couldn't go off the deep end. I could just say, "Girl, if I wasn't saved, I would cuss somebody out and not blink an eye!"

Chapter 9
FLAT CHAMPAGNE

Imagine this scenario. You go to Happy Hour after work. You are there to support your friend who called you up and said she needed a drink. She had a hard day and was venting about her crazy boss.

You hear her frustrations, but instead of telling her to "rebuke the Devil" and "just call on Jesus, for He will answer prayer," you actually listen to what is really bothering your friend. You want to know more about what is going on with her.

She confides in you. Her husband wants to get a divorce. Her son is a straight-A student, but his grades are slipping. She has been going to work and handling her assignments without getting any acknowledgment from her boss, her husband, or her family. Nobody really has asked her how she feels. But all she wants is some peace and some relief from all the stress and the guilt and the hurt.

You offer her some really good resources that you've found helped you. Some books on forgiveness and rebuilding self-esteem.

Saved, Sanctified and Still Need a Drink!

Ways to help process marriage and divorce. A good article on coping with stress and understanding depression. You even suggest that she might want to see a therapist or an acupuncturist. You know someone who is good with helping women with transitional issues.

She bristles. "I've been taught that if you can't find peace in the Lord and just studying the Word of God to get the answers, then everything else out there is just false doctrines."

"How is that working for you?" you ask her.

She is silent. But she orders another drink.

. . . .

During the '90s, I watched a lot of bubbles burst. O.J Simpson. Bill Clinton. Magic Johnson. Princess Diana. Clarence Thomas. Catholic priests. Elijah Muhammad.

I saw and felt the same kinds of experiences in my own life. I realized that the "inside" people did a lot of the "outside" things but were good about hiding what they were doing. I felt the loss of innocence about religion, church, and holiness.

It was a sad and confusing time in my life. I struggled to get some clarity. That's when I went to counseling. I needed a drink, and I literally went straight to the wine bottle. I became a heavy wine drinker. Although I masked my own drinking around "being a wine connoisseur," I was a "closeted winebibber-almost-alcoholic-black-woman-about-ready-to-call-it-a-day"!

I remained the "good Christian girl" in my head, while I steadily got blindsided. Cheatings, infidelities, secret babies, hidden affairs, domestic abuse, backstabbers, haters. Everything we in the "saved and sanctified" world called "The Enemy, the Devil, and Satan" was tied up in all the behaviors. But the only thing was that these were people who, on the outside, professed to be Christians!

Flat Champagne

I now could relate to my father. I was the same age as he was when he got saved—in my thirties. I was unhappy, drinking, and lost inside. I was tired of no peace. Of people telling me things that weren't true. Of being taken advantage of, and being disappointed, feeling guilty, and covering up lies.

The only difference was that I was already saved. I didn't need to go find a church late at night and "turn myself in" to the Lord. What I needed was something more personal. I needed to know myself.

I remembered the church teaching that Jesus provided to people looking for spiritual solution. And guess what? It was a drink!

He called it "living water."

When I stopped all the guilt and accepted myself just as I was, I gained a different perspective on life and my purpose, and it allowed me to reframe things. I had to turn away from all the fear and judgment so I could settle into a life of serenity and peace. Who knew that my spiritual awakening would be so dramatic, yet so simple? As my father used to say, "It's so easy, it's hard!" Deep.

You may agree. Or not. It doesn't matter to me. All I know is, if you are still reading this book, you have an opinion. Still judging me and others? Still judging yourself? Keep reading—it gets deeper!

Chapter 10

INVISIBLE DRUNKS

Imagine this scenario. You just found out that a high school classmate of yours passed away. You are shocked because he was so young. After you inquire on Facebook, you get the information about where the funeral will be held. The least you can do is go and pay your respects.

You attend the funeral at his home church. You didn't know he belonged to a holiness church. When you look at the program, you see his picture on the cover and read the obituary. He was very active in his church. He was a Sunday School teacher and a choir director. His father was one of the founders of the church, and he seemed to come from a long legacy of saved and sanctified leaders.

The obituary doesn't say how he died. It also doesn't mention any direct survivors. No wife, no kids. He was in his forties. Didn't he ever get married?

When you watch the line of people walking past to view his body, there are two men who go up. They are obviously "together." They are holding hands and silently weeping. The rest of the church members walk around the men. You see how awkward they feel. They seem a little embarrassed that these two men would even have the audacity to hold hands, let alone be up at the casket crying.

As you listen to the pastor of the church give the eulogy, you notice that he never talks about your friend "going home to be with the Lord." He talks more about the mother and how "the church is praying for her in her time of sorrow."

So, now you are curious. You ask the person next to you: "Was he gay or something?" The person you asked rolls her eyes. "Yes, but nobody ever talked about it at church. We all just knew. We think he died of AIDS, but nobody ever said that is what it was."

After you walk out of the service, you feel a deep sense of loss. It seemed that, for all the years your friend belonged to that church, he was never validated, especially at the moment when it mattered most. Instead of going home to be with the Lord, he was the "elephant in the room."

Somehow though, you could imagine his spirit watching over the service, looking at all the hypocrites and laughing before he took off for heaven.

With a drink in his hand.

· · · · · · ·

The holiness churches are no different from other religious cultures when it comes to hypocrisy. Jesus talked about it a lot, and it seemed that, of all the behaviors He hated, it wasn't drinking or smoking or having a baby out of wedlock that He hated the most. It was hypocrisy.

Invisible Drunks

The previous scenario illustrates what I mean. Here is a man who had attended his church all of his life. He participated in the services. He read his Bible. He loved the Lord. But he was also a gay man. He could have been an alcoholic and been treated better than he was treated at his funeral. In the church, being silently ignored is worse than being openly condemned.

Why does this issue resonate with me so strongly? In 1990, I was thirty-seven years old, working as a public health professional during the height of the AIDS epidemic. That is when I struggled with my religious upbringing as it related to the gay community. At that time, I had friends who had grown up in the holiness church who were contracting the virus. They were being ostracized by the Black community and by the Christian community. The "saved and sanctified" were the worst judges. Many of the pastors wouldn't even address it. It was an uncomfortable subject to bring up in the pulpit.

Why? Go back to the questionnaire. Can you be saved and sanctified and still be gay? If you said "No," then you see why the pastor couldn't preach a "homegoing" message. He would have to admit that this man could go to heaven. If you said "Yes," then you would have to admit that it is OK to be gay and be saved. What pastor was ready to say that out loud?

As messed up as it seems now, it was AIDS that opened the door to discuss homosexuality in the Black church. I remember my father asking me something that shocked me. He recognized that I was a health educator. That was my job. I was talking AIDS prevention to all kinds of groups. He called me to invite me to his district meeting in Spokane, Washington, to do a presentation to his congregation. I wasn't a missionary or a church leader. What did he want me to talk to his congregation about?

"AIDS," he said. I was stunned. "Why me?" I asked him. "Because I am the pastor. I cannot condone homosexuality. But I

Saved, Sanctified and Still Need a Drink!

know our people are dealing with it, and they need to know how to handle it. They need the education. You understand the church. You know how to talk to our folks with love and respect. Only you. I trust you to help us all understand."

Wow.

That was the first time in years that I'd participated in this "blurred lines" phase of the church: the crossing of what was "holiness" with what was "hell," in a new and enlightened way. I was honored—and scared. I had to really think about how to walk that fine line. But I did it beautifully. I was proud of myself. It was a big deal—for me and for my father.

How many "elephant in the room" situations have you seen in the church? What would Jesus do? Even more importantly, what would *you* do?

Chapter 11
GOOD SPIRITS

It is no coincidence that "spirits" is a common name for alcoholic beverages. The feelings that come from drinking alcohol range from mild to severe. From "buzzed" to "blackout." I have felt them all.

Guilt, condemnation, fear, shame, embarrassment. I struggled with these feelings all of my life. After many years of living "in sin," I couldn't take it anymore. I was tired of suffering inside. Since I wasn't comfortable talking to people or getting any outside help, I used journaling to explore my deep questions and my painful emotions.

I remember feeling very confused about ten years ago. I sat down and began to write all of my feelings down, as usual. But this time, I took a different approach. Instead of starting with the date of my journal entry, I just wrote at the top of a blank page these two words: "SPIRIT SAYS..." Then, I waited. I figured that if there was a HOLY GHOST, it was time to get its divine guidance. I asked the Spirit to reveal itself to me in my writing. And *She* did!

I started writing. It *was* me, but it *wasn't* "me." And no, it was not this booming male voice from out of nowhere. It was *my spirit*! I had never thought to ask Her to talk to me before. I guess I always assumed the spiritual voice was not a female, but a male. Like how I imagined White Jesus would sound if he were to speak to me. Or like I imagined the Holy Ghost to break out in "other tongues" that I wouldn't recognize.

Instead, *She* came forth. What a wonderful discovery—to channel my own Spirit's voice. I imagined that my father had the same feeling when he knew God was speaking directly to him back in 1960. I believed my father's story of his conversion because he was so adamant about it. He probably heard his own Spirit speaking to him at that moment. But when it happened to me, it was different. It was not so dramatic. It was peaceful. Quiet. Beautiful. Soothing. And real. The calming presence that so many people say I exude. It is my Spirit!

My Spirit's voice expressed in my journals! Wow! I dare you to try it! Just ask. Call it forth! And write down what comes to you. It is different. It is another voice, and it is there! Just pay attention, and let it speak through you. The words that come out will be comforting, encouraging, and loving. No judgment. No criticism. No fear. No anger. Powerful insight!

From then on, I would continue the practice, and loved it! It helped me to open my heart and expand the range of how I viewed spiritual concepts. My personal journey broadened. I learned so much from reading other books. I talked to other people who did not come from the "saved and sanctified" cultural background like I did, but who had deep insights about God and spiritual truths. The exposure was great!

In time, I developed a newfound appreciation for the wisdom of my African-American spiritual culture as well as other cultures. Having worked in the public health field for more than thirty years and, specifically, interacting with all kinds of cultural communities, I had already gained so much insight into other world views. I was exposed to the wisdom of Native American elders, the *curanderas* of some Hispanic cultures, the beliefs and perspectives of people who came from the Islamic traditions, the Hindu and Buddhist backgrounds, the Catholics, the Yoruba, the Jewish, and the various Christian faiths and sects. I even appreciated the atheists who could not wrap their heads around the existence of a God. It didn't matter. All humans were searching for the same thing. Acceptance. Understanding. Love. And being who they wanted to be, without judgment. Without fear. Without guilt.

I finally forgave myself, others, and even my "saved and sanctified" stereotypes that had gripped me for so long. I let it all go. I learned the importance of surrender. Not *giving up*, mind you—just releasing a lot of the guilt, the judgment, the fear. And like my Spirit, I became aware of everything around me. I understood what it meant to "be *in* the world, but not *of* the world!"

Most importantly, I came to know that what we call *love* is *not a feeling*. It is *power*. A universal *force*. A *change agent*.

Now, "saved, sanctified…and still need a drink…" is just my way of saying that we all go through the journey. When we "need a drink," our energy is showing us where we are in the process.

Chapter 12

EAT, DRINK, AND BE MERRY!

The last scenario brings me full circle. I wrote this book to bring awareness. It was not enough for me to "just pray" and "read the Bible" to feel peace. There are so many people who are told to do this, but it doesn't solve the problem. You may be like I was—still guilty and confused about your beliefs and your feelings. Just know that you are not alone! It is the state that many of us are still in. If you are reading this book, then you have an opportunity to heal and to help others heal.

Self-discovery work has become my passion because of my "saved and sanctified" journey. If you are on a journey of self-discovery, I recommend that you find excellent support for yourself and your friends or family members who struggle with the issues

I talked about in this book. It helps to know we are all in this together—with love, not judgment.

I went through a fifty-year journey just to write this book the way I did. I had to go all the way back to the beginning just to put things into perspective. What I have now that I didn't have when I was younger is *wisdom* and *understanding*.

> *"When wisdom entereth into thine heart, and knowledge is pleasant unto thy soul; Discretion shall preserve thee; understanding shall keep thee."*
> — PROVERBS 2:10-11

Now that I have these, I *love* God, and, more importantly, I *love* myself as I *am*. I *love* my history. I *love* the Church of God in Christ. I *love* the saints and the sinners. I *love* White Jesus and Black Jesus. I *love* the services that touch my Spirit. I *love* gospel music, but I also *love* any music that communicates to my heart. I *love the values I learned:* FAITH, SURRENDER, HEALING, FORGIVENESS, PRAYER, INSPIRATION, *and* HOPE!

I found that I have a personal relationship with God, through my Spirit. She speaks to me and through me, especially when I am still, quiet, and alert. I *love her*! And she loves me deeply.

What I learned to do most of all was *love*! I learned to pay attention to my unique energy, which is the *Holy Spirit*. I stopped identifying with "labels and name tags" like "saved, sanctified, and filled with the Holy Ghost." Those words did not define who I was in the world anymore. Nor did they define my relationship with God.

I came to better understand the spiritual meanings of the Biblical scriptures because they match my *wisdom*. It took my own journey of growth and maturity to fully grasp what the teachings mean.

I can discern who has gained wisdom now. Those are the ones I listen to, and, absorb their insights.

I practice daily meditation. I journal every day and have been journaling for decades. I have kept my journals. They are my best teacher about who I am, because they don't lie. I know exactly how to tap into my spiritual guide, and it is not by "speaking in tongues." It is by giving my Spirit a chance to express herself through my journaling and through the energy centers in my body. When she communicates with me, it is always loving. Never harsh. Never mean. Never judgmental. But always right!

And I know when I do call on Jesus, *He will answer prayer*! I just had to learn how to recognize it in my personal journey with God. It is *so much better now*!

In Conclusion...Let's All Go Have a Drink!

Now, aren't you glad you read my book? It wasn't so bad, was it? Maybe now you can look up and smile again. Encourage yourself and your friends and family. Tell your "saved and sanctified" friends to relax. We all *"need a drink,"* because we are all in this together!

I want to summarize the insights I hope you gained from my experience.

- There are so many ways that people feel conflicted. The expressions we use to show our struggle can be mixed in with our need to show we are also striving to live right, do right, and be our "highest" selves, even when we aren't perfect.

- Our guilt, fears, and shame can be addressed easily when we confess what we really feel inside and own up to our issues.

- We all need to recognize that some of our choices and decisions are shaped by our upbringing, and, until we get clear about what we really believe, we live a life of confusion and doubt.

- It's normal to question our beliefs. We don't have to be afraid of going to hell for that. It's OK to recognize what makes sense to you and what doesn't.

- We all have the ability to change our points of view and still keep our self-integrity. We do not need to judge others and waste our time worrying about their behavior. Everyone has to go through their own process of learning and growing, so they can gain experience and wisdom. We have no control over other people's journeys.

- There are so many opportunities for us to support and help others who need us to listen to them, without judgment, but with love and sincerity. We can understand people better when we understand their story. Which means we have to be open to hearing them when they tell us.

- We are so blessed when we can come to acceptance and love for ourselves and others, and grow as human beings. Our faith helps us to do just that.

- There is a great gift that resides in all of us—our own energy and intuition. It is there for us to know. It is time for us to tap into it more and use it.

Eat, Drink, and Be Merry!

When I sat down to write this book, I didn't know that my "saved and sanctified" journey would bring me to this level of insight. I still find myself watching people's behaviors today and thinking about what would have happened to me if I did certain things when I was growing up. I can't even imagine how I would have handled all the things that kids today have to navigate, especially in the age of social media and reality TV!

But I get over it quickly and just laugh. I realize that Jesus really doesn't judge us. We judge ourselves. The Creator still may "snatch us by the collar" to get our attention, but it is not to condemn us to hell. It's to bring us to love and peace. Whatever "saved and sanctified" looks like today, it may not look that way in the future. And I'm OK with that. It just means we are human! And that's alright with me!

Can I get an "Amen!"?

Chapter 13
NOT TO LEAVE YOU HANGING—THE NIGHTCAP!

Now that you've read the book, let me give you my response to the issues I raised at the beginning that made you laugh. Come up with your own, even if you don't agree with my answers. Just what makes sense for you is the most important thing.

- You still secretly wrestle with underlying feelings of guilt about going outside of your saved and sanctified church's teachings. You read your Bible, but you also have a copy of *A Course in Miracles* on your nightstand, and stay home to watch Eckhart Tolle on Oprah's *Super Soul Sunday*® with a mimosa, when you should be in Sunday School.

Something to think about: God is a Spirit. We are all seekers of the Spirit. Maybe God is saying the same thing in different ways. Why be afraid to learn? Other insights may make more sense to you. Just like when you go to church and hear different interpretations of the same scripture by different speakers. You get another perspective—which enriches your understanding. The Universe is infinite, and, so, why be limited?

- **You struggle with "training up your child in the way he/she should go" when you know that you strayed from the training that you were taught as a child. You fear admitting that you were not a perfect saint and did some things under the table. Your kids or family members would be shocked to find out that you really did have a drink!**

Be honest! With yourself first! Your children would be so relieved to know that you were not perfect and that you still aren't. But the worst thing is to say one thing and do another. Actions do speak louder than words. If you tell your kids to do as you say, but not as you do—they know. So trying to correct them and make them saints because you want them to be like you does not give them the opportunity to discover what is right for them.

- **You still think that you've disappointed yourself, God, Jesus, your parents, the church because you backslid, but yet you love the Lord, and no one understands how you feel. You carry a lot of guilt because of something you did, someone you betrayed, or something you lied about.**

That is because you still believe that being saved depends on your behavior. It doesn't. The whole point of Jesus's sacrifice is to release us from that belief. Everything that we absorb about how we should live, what is right and what is wrong, what is sinful and what is holy, is what keeps us from being free. Once I found out that I did not have to trip on my behavior, then I could relax and accept the grace of salvation. It is free!

> ✦ **You are tired of judgmental messages that don't make sense to you, and it just doesn't feel good to say you're saved and sanctified when you see so much mess in the church. The main ones who are shouting, preaching, testifying, and saying they are so saved seem to be the worst devils. But they get away with it. That's just not right.**

Then stop participating in messes and stop supporting judgmental message givers! It may be your home church that you've been attending since God was a baby, but if your church isn't working for you anymore, then leave. Or, just take it in stride, and get what good you can out of the experience. Watch for opportunities to show forgiveness, compassion, and just say to yourself, "These saved and sanctified folks just still need a drink!" Don't get caught up in the mess.

> ✦ **You spend a lot of your energy bemoaning the state of the church and the fact that these unseasoned pastors and untrained members really don't know what "saved and sanctified" really represents, because they let anyone and everyone come in and do whatever they want. What happened to the standards? Where's the *"Come out of the world and be ye separate"* part of holiness?**

The Church is an institution. Just like most institutions, they have their hierarchies and their politics. You can't be a leader without followers. Look at the big picture. It is so interesting that those who are not authentic and sincere usually fall by the wayside, sooner or later. Even though a lot of the superficial things have changed, the true depth of the message of salvation and forgiveness and connection to God's grace remains the same. So just relax. Live the way you know is right for you.

- ✦ You feel that "saved and sanctified" is too commercialized and made to be comical and funny. You are concerned about the image of the Black church being tied to *Madea Goes to Jail*. Isn't it important to represent your faith in a way that others take you seriously? When others come to your church who don't understand your quirky members, you feel embarrassed and ashamed that Brother Roscoe will pick that Sunday to act a fool. That just plays into the stereotypes.

Don't you just love your people? You know how we are, how we act, how we deal, and yes, we are comical and funny. But we are also very devout, sincere, spiritual, and powerful. There is absolutely nothing to be ashamed of, because we express ourselves, and everyone is accepted for who they are. The only change I would love to see in our churches is that we affirm and love everybody instead of laughing at them behind their backs or putting them down to others.

- ✦ You are confused, ashamed, or indifferent as to what your "saved and sanctified" history represents in your life. You grew up with it, the rest of your family is still in it, but you don't want to claim it for yourself. You feel like you've

Not to Leave You Hanging—the Nightcap!

disappointed your family, and you still crave their acceptance, even though you don't claim to be "saved and sanctified."

Embrace your "saved and sanctified" history! It is rich, beautiful, and sacred! There is nothing else like it in the world! Where else can you feel the power of the anointing of God when everyone is in one accord, as stated in Acts 2:4? How can you doubt the changes that you see in the truly converted, knowing how they were before they got saved? The gospel music we sing is the most powerful music on the planet. We have so much blood, sweat, tears, joy, peace, and hope wrapped up in our DNA! So, yes, you may be "saved, sanctified and still need a drink," but the Spirit of God fills us all with more than anything on earth could satisfy. That is why we prevail, and that is what we know to be true!

Notes and Reflections

Notes and Reflections

Notes and Reflections

Notes and Reflections

Notes and Reflections

ABOUT THE AUTHOR

Barbara Freeman is an accomplished "Wisdom Woman" who is passionate about self-discovery work. She keeps track of her life's journey through her decades-long practice of journaling. Having had a long and successful career as a public health professional, she now enjoys her private consulting practice, which includes mentoring aspiring nonprofit entrepreneurs and community leaders. She is known for generously sharing her knowledge and wisdom with others. Her website is *www.thewisdomwoman.com*.

www.ingramcontent.com/pod-product-compliance
Lightning Source LLC
Chambersburg PA
CBHW022228010526
44113CB00033B/743